THE TASTE OF WILD WATER

Poems and Stories Found While Walking in Woods

PICTORES OPERIS,
Heinricus Füllmaurer.   Albertus Meyer.

Books by Stephen Harrod Buhner

Sacred Plant Medicine

One Spirit Many Peoples

Sacred and Herbal Healing Beers

Herbal Antibiotics

Herbs for Hepatitis C and the Liver

The Lost Language of Plants

Vital Man

The Fasting Path

The Secret Teachings of Plants

The Natural Testosterone Plan

The Taste of Wild Water

Inhabiting the Word (in press)

THE TASTE OF WILD WATER

Poems and Stories Found While Walking in Woods

Fr Jonathan
for the journey

by Stephen Harrod Buhner

Raven Press

Silver City, New Mexico

Portions of this book have appeared in the books *Sacred Plant Medicine, The Lost Language of Plants, Inhabiting the Word,* and *The Secret Teachings of Plants.* Some of the poems have appeared in *Poetry Motel* and *Sacred Fire.* An earlier form of the book was published online in 2003.

p.:cm.
ISBN 978-0-9708696-1-6
"An earlier form of the book was published online in 2003."—
T.p. verso

1. Nature, Healing power of—Poetry. 2. Nautre in literature. 3. Spiritual life—Poetry. 4. Ecstasy in literature. I. Title

PS3602.U366 T37 2009
811/.6—dc22   0906

First Edition
Raven Press
8 Pioneer Road
Silver City, New Mexico 88061

Dedication

For my great-grandparents,

C.G. and Mary Burney Harrod

Acknowledgments

Robert Bly, Dale Pendell, Patrick Pritchett, Trishuwa,

Toni Knapp.

TABLE OF CONTENTS

Section One - Veriditas

Section Two - The Fruitful Darkness

Section Three - The Taste of Wild Water

Section Four - Grains of Sand From Another Shore

ONE

Veriditas

WALKING

More than once

I have walked

in deep forest

searching for the path

that lay concealed

beneath my feet.

DISTURBED BY WIND

A two-thousand-year-old tree

in an ecosystem filled

with a

    tumultuous,

        complex,

            riot

            of interacting plant species

    feels

markedly different

than a lone sapling

surrounded by grass,

stark in the front yard

of a new housing development,

or the Norfolk pine

leaning drunkenly

in the corner of the kitchen.

The   green,

        orderly

        lawns

surrounding children's homes
do not bear any relationship
    to the up-and-down,
        uneven landscapes
            filled with giant, craggy outcroppings
          of the immeasurably ancient stones of Earth
    that wild landscapes often possess.

A calm pond lends us serenity,
yet when its waters
are disturbed
                by wind
are we not also disturbed?
our emotions unsettled?

Where is it
        that our feelings
               really come from?

LEAF TAKING

As Earth leaves,

we remain,

stones,

not plants,

not green,

tiny pebbles

scattered

on an empty street.

A THOUGHT

Thomas Huxley,

Darwin's strongest defender,

observed

that "No rational man,

cognizant of the facts,

believes that the Negro

is the equal

still less the superior,

of the white man."

The assertion

that the degree of rational "thinking"

of any species

is illustrative of its position

on the ladder of evolutionary hierarchy

is only a decision

by an organism

(and specific people)

with a vested interest

in what is being decided.

What does
		a bristlecone pine
				do
		during six thousand years
of life?

What does
		a blue whale
				do
		with the largest brain
on Earth?

PLANT MEDICINE

for angelica

Do you think it possible to dissect a human being,

render it down into its constituent parts,

feed those into a machine which measures such things

and determine from that

its ability to paint or create great music?

No?

Then why do you think

that once you have done this with my body

you know anything about me?

COYOTE

There was a time
when I saw the world
coyote lives in.

I had walked up,
with a friend - once upon a time,
behind the rocks,
the big ones that rise up, mossy-greened,
and cradle the forest-shadowed ponds
that the ducks and moose love,
to seek the slight-sloping, grassy meadow hidden behind
them.

We half-lay for hours
in the tall emerald grass
amongst the ancient trees that towered over
the drifting textures of the land.
While our elbows supported us
we talked of plants,
and stones,
and the wisdom of moss.   9

Slowly we began,
as humans sometimes do,
to slip into the wildness of the world.
Our language began to slow
down, pause, and falter.
Into silence we drifted
and for some reason
that only our souls understood that day
we flowed with it, not talking.

Colors became more vivid
and the air began to sparkle.
Our breathing and the sounds of forest
took on a luminous quality.
And into this silence coyote ambled,
following a game trail
that flowed, brown runnel, near our feet.

Her tongue lolled out
the side of her mouth,
and she was laughing
that crazy laugh coyote has,

10

while her eyes spun
as she watched the dancing bones
that lie under the fabric of the world.

Crazy, gamboling coyote.
Third force in Universe.
I said under my breath,
"Turn your head to the right."
And my friend sat up
and said, "What?"
And in so doing, lost her chance to see.

I, still watching, saw Coyote's eyes
shift out of that crazy, spinning universe
and shocked,

no,

betrayed,

by the secrecy of our immersion
she flipped straight up and over
and ran, tail between her legs,
only some strange kind of dog,
up the trail.

What I glimpsed through coyote's eyes
lodged in a part of my brain
I did not know I had.
I can reach out and touch it sometimes.
My eyes begin to spin,
and I feel a bit dizzy,
and I can see
dancing bones
under the fabric of the world.

I still do not know
what the world
that coyote lives in
when no one is watching
does
but I do know it is ancient
far beyond the species lifetime of humans
and that next to it, *our* world
is only a chip of wood
floating on the ocean.

HOMECOMING

There is one place

in all the Universe

that has been made

just for you.

And it is inside

your own

feet.

TWO

The Fruitful Darkness

BLACK WINGS

Why is it
my unkindnesses
are so poignantly remembered
while the interiors of
remembered kindnesses
remain so emotionally empty?

My childish bullet
entering the chest of the crow
The shocked realization of my lie
pooling in the eyes of my beloved

I remember the cry,
then the stillness,
black wings taking her away,
seeking a past she would never find,
deeper in the heart of the forest.

THE SHEATH

Was it your love that put this here
or the small secret part of you
that you hide in darkness?

Both smile enticingly,
hands spontaneously lifted
to touch my cheeks.

But I have noticed,
that that one's teeth
are slightly longer.

And she looks slyly
out of the corner of your eye
as she takes the sharpened words,

and slides them home
in the part of me
that love has made defenseless.

FINDING YOUNG MEN IN MANASSAS FOREST

There is a sound in war that stays in the mind and will not let go the soul of a man. When the men around you are wounded there is a sigh, or a sob, that comes up out of them—it sounds like a soft wind on a summer's day but it has a meaning in it that a summer wind will never have. You think maybe it's your imagination but you begin to listen for it and then you realize it comes out of the wounded. It comes out of them and into you and you carry it inside you until you die and maybe it doesn't let you go even then.

Later, after the fighting is done, when the cannons have ceased their awful thunder, for a little while a silence as deep as the farthest reaches of space falls upon everything left alive. Those that fortune has allowed to live, and it was through nothing unique that they possess, nothing which better men, fallen around them, did not also possess, suffer from the silence. It falls upon them in thick blankets and for a minute stuffs their eyes and ears and all their senses with its fabric. Then, too soon, the cries and whimpers and the terrible mewling of the wounded, tear the silence into fragments that remain, if at all, only in the memory.

18

There are the calls for water, the calls for a help that can never come, the calls for the sweet mothering that young men knew in a simpler time, the prayers for death. Into the living men the cries travel and they lodge in the deep recesses and will not let them go; they will hear them for as long as they live.

Around the shattered promise of these young men who will never marry, who will never bring children into the world, who will never see the look of love in a young child's eye, who will never speak with the voice of age to the next generation, lie the remains of the land, crops that will never know the harvest, the bodies of wild things that did not flee fast enough the rage of men locked in ancient struggle, great trees whose thousand years are ground into an hour's splinters, orchards that will never know the laughter of a child's swing. All lie in disarray around the wet bundles of mothers' pride and love. Then, after awhile, there is an odor that, with the sounds, enters into the living and there leaves a smudge that no amount of washing will erase. And the graves that are hurriedly dug are simple ones and shallow.

Those who survive carry a bond between them too deep for words. It is a bond that goes beyond the weakness of flesh and blood and sinew. It binds them to each other in a brotherhood that knows no limitation of space or time. And later, when they meet each other on the street or in another city or another state or another decade a silent knowledge passes between them. The knowledge passes over and around the crowds within which they walk and enters in at the eyes. There is a momentary pause as each man feels the thing enter them; they pause under its influence or stumble slightly in their walk. Then they might nod or stop a minute to speak together. And as the years pass the men feel the bond as keenly but time helps the bearing of it; the pause becomes less noticeable to any who care to look for it.

The men of Manassas knew all these things though they wished they did not. Sometimes, late in the night, the smells and the cries and the sound of men being wounded around them would take hold of them and drag them gasping and wretched to the shores of consciousness. There they would lie sweating, calming themselves, and they would understand that the stamp of strangeness that Civil War had placed upon them would never pass until they themselves had passed, until they met once again those comrades who had gone before.

THE SADNESS OF OLD MEN

Never to touch
such a throat again,
never to lie nestled
in the curve of such an arm,
one leg thrown over another,
desire hard and throbbing,
male pollen seeking passage,
locked in perfumed
and moist embrace,
crying out
amongst the petals of her hair,
hands clenched tightly
together
as she releases that sound
from deep inside her,
that joins with mine.
Oh God! *Never.*

LONGING

Who was it that injured you?

      Were you very young?

You must have been, for

      I see your mouth moving

seeking a nipple,

      or some sustenance from life,

that a deeper part of you

      has longed for,

but has never been able to find.

I wake in the night sometimes

      and find you curled

in the shadow of my arm.

      Feet drawn up, thumb sucking

and it takes an effort

      to pull the wrinkled member

from my mouth

      to relax my legs

and straighten them out

under the cold,

      emptiness

      of the sheets.

THE WAITING

They call them night mares,

those horses our souls ride

through the darkness that surrounds us

when our conscious minds sleep.

We do not reign there

they control themselves

or perhaps they respond to commands

known only to powers

that science says do not exist,

powers that hide silent in the night,

in a place where reason has no weight,

and an ancient intelligence still rules.

So, we wake, sweating,

and look to Freud,

or Jung,

or biochemistry,

and speak platitudes to ourselves,

or take a little pill,

to try and conquer powers

that hover at the edges of our world

waiting, as they have patiently done,

since before we were born,

and as they will continue to do

long after we are gone.

DARKNESS

You cannot know what awaits you
until you surrender and enter the darkness.
It may be that the sun shines there,
that the grass is green,
that your family awaits you
as they have been waiting,
for years upon years
of a length your sleeping self cannot imagine.

It is in the surrender
and in the turning to meet the darkness
that freedom lies.
For we are dead already,
only vague memories
in times we cannot imagine,
shadows in dusty books
moldering on distant shelves,
touched by hands
that cannot know
the fullness of our lives.　25

There is no place so dark

that the one who loves thee

and who has been set here to help thee

has not already been

and prepared thy place.

THREE

The Taste of Wild Water

THE TASTE OF WILD WATER

I was eight the first time I tasted wild water.

I lay with my great-grandfather along the bank of a pond deep in rural Indiana. I was close enough that his smell came strongly to me, subtly shading and comforting the wild smells surrounding me. It was a smell that I have known since I have known smell, deeply encoded in my body-memory, stored away with other body-memories that are bound together with the origins of my life: the feel of his starched shirts against my newborn skin, the smell of his soap and cigarettes, and his voice a deep rumble into which was interwoven the communications of ancient generations and nineteenth-century life.

My great-grandmother is there in body-memory, too. Her voice throaty. She overweight and chain-smoking, hard-drinking and peering nearsighted, heavy-bosomed, strongly perfumed. And always with her memory are smells of gravy and fried chicken, green beans boiled to non-existence, the taste of too-sweet iced tea in great, sweating glass jugs.

And the feeling of being loved deep into the soul till it matters not the shape of a person's body or the irregularities of their personality.

I remember journeys to their formal stately home in Columbus: dark and dangerous basements, attics filled with memories and old smells, mirrors that distorted new generations peering half-frightened into them, and overstuffed horsehair chairs that could not be sat upon without sliding off. And out back of the house, my great-grandfather's office where patients from the nineteenth century came to see their doctor.

Those patients had little trust in the new generation of physicians that peered condescendingly down at them, talking as if to children, certain of their educational pedigree, all in clean-white-shining-characterless faces. They came instead to be with a fellow traveler through time, who had been filled with stories of Civil War, begun life on horses and in buggies, had seen them die in one world war and then another. One who used the old medicines and still looked at the tongue, who palpated the organs, and who said, "Say 'ahhh.'"

I sometimes went in the back door of that office –
drawn always against my will. It stood darkly in the back of
the garden, pulling on me, until I could resist no longer. Then
uncertain, trembling, I would walk past the goldfish pond
filled with ancient flashing carp, along the overgrown
walkway, to the blond brick building with the dark brown
door. Even touching the handle brought its smell to the
nostrils: old metal and years of human touch. The knob
rattled slightly, but it took a pressure to turn it, for the door
fit tightly. All of my strength was necessary and my hand
would just start to slip when the door would let go with a
sudden "thunk" and pop open a little. More smells would
come, smells held at bay behind blond brick, peeling brown
door, metal latch and knob. Strange smells: of herbal
medicines and chemicals and leather, of oak and old paper, of
old sickness and pain, and of the years of human lives, which
has a smell all its own.

The door creaked when I pulled it open, hinges
protesting, and it scraped along the concrete walk. When it
was finally open there was always that terrible moment when I

had to decide whether or not to step inside. In the dim light lay old boxes and metal things, wornout brooms, and scrapes on the walls, and that slightly damp concrete with its own wetly penetrating smell. As I breathed it in I was caught up and carried away to some kind of life that I did not understand. It seemed so old and somehow so sad that I could hardly take breath. But none of these things came to me in words. They expressed themselves in the instinctive motions of flight, half turning to the door again to go, to get away, to feel once again the sunlight play over my body and fill up my lungs. And sometimes I gave it rein and left not-running, remembering to close the door, to push on it until it snicked into place. And somehow in the back of my mind I could hear a sad thing crying out to me - a thing that I could not hold, could not understand, could not bear.

But other times I would not turn and go, not give that silent fear expression or control over my body. I would reach out and turn on the light and sometimes I would even close the door behind me and place myself firmly in that world. Then, trembling, I would step out into it and it would close about me firmly, insistently, irrevocably.

Along the right side of the room were counters and above them shelves. In the middle of the counter was a large sink, stained by fearful liquids over unimaginable years. On the shelves above were brown bottles leaning, filled, leaking, mysterious, and strange. The smell was strong - of herbal medicines, and chemicals, and water, and plants, and age. Along the left side of the room were shelves filled with boxes and bottles and metal devices and things that my memory provides no shapes for.

Once I had made it this far, it was seldom that I did not go on. There was a door ahead of me and through it the room where my great-grandfather saw his patients. It was a room that felt safe, touched by human life. There was a high leather table with shiny metal things at one end that looked like stirrups or the spurs used by cowboys. There was a desk with a chair and papers and the walls were clean and it smelled like hospitals and fear and hope all at the same time.

At the far wall there was another door, always closed. It carried on its surface a shiny patina of age, the knob turned silently and easily and on the other side was the waiting room.

There was a couch, its leather dark with years, its oak body rubbed black and smooth. There were oak chairs and end tables with magazines and table lamps and along the front length of the couch there was a low table and on it a large glass jar, perhaps a foot across. It was filled with shark teeth and I knew I could take off the top and reach inside and take some if I wanted. Sometimes I did and wondered about a fish that could have these kind of teeth and sometimes I would think about falling in the ocean - but not often.

Eventually I would turn and retrace my steps and always that back room would challenge me. I would snake through it quickly, hearing soft footfalls behind me that I could not turn and face and it always seemed that I got the door closed just in time. I would shake then and not understand why I had ventured in and it might be a month or a year before I did it again.

They had another house - in the country.

It was in Columbus that I was introduced to the mysteries of my great-grandfather's profession but in the Indiana forests of his country home that I was introduced to the mysteries of the human and the Earth and of the interior world that all human beings possess.

His country house was a hand-hewn, oak barn built a century before. My great-grandfather had bought it, numbered the pieces, disassembled it, moved it to the farm and rebuilt it. I remember visits there, lying next to him in bed and hearing his stories. It did not matter what he said but only the sound and rhythms of his voice, his arm about me, and his smell sinking deep within me. I remember one night lying with him when the story was done and looking up from slitted eyelids to his face and knowing that the only thing I wanted in life was to be a man like this man. Only years later did I realize the Universe hears such requests and shapes irrevocable destiny from child thought. Even more years passed before I realized that there is a price to granted wishes.

Sometimes he would take me out into the woods on that farm and we would walk. There is a special kind of shadow that happens in deep woods that are old and have been left undisturbed. Underneath the canopy of ancient hardwood trees the greens are deeper, the soil blacker, the smells richer. And there is a shadow that is over everything, calling out that there is a deeper world than the human of which we are a part. Something came out of that place and entered my body. I felt more whole, more human, more loved, more a part of the world. And in some indefinable way I *knew* who I was.

I remember the particular way my great-grandfather walked through those woods - few walk that way now. I see it mostly in old pictures, in the stance of ancient ancestors, of Civil War veterans, of people long gone. That way of walking has a particular smell, a particular gait, a particular rhythm, a particular integration with Earth and plant and water. As we walked through those woods he would push aside a plant in his path, but it was not brusquely done. Rather he moved them from his path as if they were relatives he was setting aside. The soil was black with a bit of clay and it could be easily formed with the hands. A shovel would go in deeply and there were few stones. The roots of the plants entwined in that deep dark soil and our feet sank down a little as we walked - as if we were moving on the living tension of the soil, like the water spiders that skated on the pond where we fished. My great-grandfather's feet knew the tension of that soil - they expected it and the soles of his feet spoke to it, conversed with Earth, each step of the way.

When we reached the pond, we would lie for hours on its banks, the silence a blanket over us. Sometimes we would drop a word into the silence like a stone into the water and the word's meaning would send ripples through us until they ebbed, slowed, and stopped. Still, even then I knew those words were unnecessary. For in our time together we were doing something without words that humans have done for millennia. As we lay with the smells and the sounds and the feels of that place deep inside something would leave his body and enter mine. I would breathe it into me as slowly as I breathed in his smell; something in my soul found purchase in it. It was a food without which I could not become human. It is always passed in silence between the man and the boy, between the woman and the girl. It is handed down from one interior world to the next. Its essence penetrates the muscles of the body, the oxygen of the blood, the substance of the spirit. And this was the time in which I first tasted wild water.

A man's hand possesses touch and touching, softness
and hardness, those deep veins on its back that capture the
eyes and will not let them go, and all his life written in the
lines of his palm. I remember lying back upon my elbows with
a piece of grass between my teeth and my great-grandfather
leaning forward and cupping his hand, sliding it under the
surface of that glassy pond. He lifted the shining surface to
my lips and said "Here, have you ever tasted this water?" I
looked at him askance and caught the gleam in his eye, then
bent my head and pursed my lips. I remember the
translucency of that water, the tiny particles of dirt floating
in its depths, and below it all his life written in the palm of
his hand. The water was sweet and cooling; my body liked it.
As I lifted my head, I caught the glint in his eye and he made
that particular gritty sound with his teeth as he smiled that I
loved so much. "Good isn't it?" he asked. And I remember
nodding. And then we lay back down and that thing
continued to come out of his body into mine.

Later, my mother caught me drinking wild water and
told me it would kill me and began to instill in me a fear of

the wildness of nature. And later still, my great-grandfather died and my days began to be filled with TV dinners and the flickering, half-intimacy of television. The years passed and the voices of my ancestors began to fade from memory; I became used to the taste of domesticated water.

It was long and long again before I tasted wild water once more, before the seeds that the land and my great-grandfather had planted within me began their slow growth. And even more years passed before I was no longer afraid wild water would kill me. The journey back to wild water is a long one.

And now, in my turn I have walked with my son in the deep forest. I have lain next to him and felt something leave my body and enter his. He needs it less often the older he becomes. Still, sometimes he is unsettled and paces the floor and a peculiar look comes over his face. Agitated, he will ask if he can lie next to me and in silence I hold him. Something in him opens up and a food flows out of me into him. The color and tone of his skin changes and his breathing slows and deepens and eventually he sighs and is filled once more.

I know that in his time he will pass this on as it was in turn passed into me. And perhaps also, one day, he will bend over and cup his hands, and ask his child or grandchild or some child:

"Here, have you ever tasted this water?"

FOUR

Grains of Sand From

Another Shore

ANCIENT HERBALS

Today I read the description
of a medicinal plant
in a seventeenth-century herbal.
The words,
in intimate detail,
described *Potentilla*
and how the author used it to heal
long, long ago.

After I closed the book
and shut out the strange, time-distorted vocabulary
I took my staff,
and walked the fields
surrounding my home.
I do not know why I paused
and looked down
to see the same *Potentilla*
three hundred years later.

The description from the book,
like an insubstantial shadow in my mind,
arranged itself
over the five jagged fingers of Potentilla's leaves,
his straggly stem,
swaying yellow flowers,
and clicked into place.

Wind,
blowing down
a million years of plant medicine
brushed against me.
I flickered and was gone,
insubstantial shadow in the mind of Earth.

And for a moment
I was an old herbalist in 1720,
brushing back my cloak with my hand
as I bent to look
at a plant
that Hippocrates had used
2000 years before me.

MOTIONLESS IN MOONLIGHT

There is no place you
are not seen.

It is no secondhand God
but the stones under your feet,
The tree leaning casual
in shadows,
the wolf motionless
in moonlight,
your own soul
standing silent in darkness
next to your unconscious self

that see you,

all of you.

In spite of your
thinking

yourself safely invisible,

these beings,

their lives,

pull,

tug,

at your tethers,

and call you back

to suckle

in leaf-dappled shadow,

at the ancient breast

that suckled humans

long before Jesus

saw light of day,

or palmed iron,

or Buddha sat,

or ate mushrooms,

or man walked

on the moon.

GLIMPSES OF THE PATTERN THAT CONNECTS

A crow -

wings sculling invisibility,

tail feathers bending and caressing currents.

A cloud -

resting on air,

bottom curving up and over the warmth of Earth.

MOUNTAINS

I heard these mountains think yesterday.

Their thoughts are as deep

and as ancient

as the wild veins of gold

that tangle shining among their toes.

They are so much slow

er than I

am

that I had some trouble

checking my headlong flight

long enough to

listen.

Many men

who lived before me

understood the thoughts

of these mountains.

Wait!

Did you hear laughing?

47

FLOWERS

Semen is Latin

for a dormant, fertilized,

plant ovum -

a seed.

Men's ejaculate

is chemically more akin

to plant pollen.

See,

it is really

more accurate to call it

mammal pollen.

To call it

semen

is to thrust an insanity

deep inside our culture:

that men plow women

and plant their seed

when, in fact,

what they are doing

is pollinating

flowers.

Now.

Doesn't that change everything between us?

CEMETERIES

When we allowed

science·to convince us

that there is no soul

or intelligence in matter,

the Earth's physical forms

became only cemetery markers

showing where spirits once moved

through the world.

The autopsy

of the material world

then began in earnest.

Its dissected parts

litter the landscape

and we walk, depressed,

among lifeless statuary,

only accidental lifeforms

on the surface of

a ball of rock

hurtling around the sun.

The metal gate is unlocked.

Other kinds of flowers

nod in sunlight

outside that wrought-iron fence.

SONG OF GENERATIONS

I am the son of white slave owners
and black maids,
dead Union soldiers
and rich plantation owners,
a signer of the Declaration of Independence
and English aristocrats.

In my body
runs the blood of Cherokee people
and implacable Indian killers,
fundamentalist Christian ministers
and Indian, Celtic, and European pagans,
powerful political physicians
who outlawed alternative medicine
and midwives and herbalists.

Irish freedom fighters and English soldiers,
Irish, Scottish, Dutch,

English, German, Austrian,
farmers and peasants, rich industrialists –
Landowners! –
all live within me.

My body is made of the soil,
rocks,
trees,
and air
of this North American land.

My mind has been formed
by human beings out of long years of history
and continents I have never seen,
my spirit forged by the hand of God,
the sweet, singing breath of the Pipe,
and the upwelling, sacred power of Earth.

The heady rhythms of tribal Africa,

diluted by ocean miles and four hundred years,
were rocked into my body
through the sweet smells and gentle walking
of my grandmothers' maids.

The songs of Ireland,
muted by distance and generations,
still sing melancholy, sacred wisdom in my blood.
The primal pipes of Scotland
call me still to stand with my people,
and Cherokee plant song
still stirs me to dawn awakening.

Over and above them all
thunders the sacred song of Universe
and of Earth.
It is a cacophony of sound
or a great symphony of the song of humankind
and the sacred
in interblended harmony.

Sometimes,

simultaneously,

it is both.

It would be easier,

perhaps,

to be the son of unblended,

tribally-pure, father and mother,

whose healthy purity

stretches back to the dawn of time.

I, their whole expression.

But there are few of us

that can make such a claim.

We play the hand

that Creator has given us.

But. . .

is there not beauty

in such a song of interblended harmonies?

Such a song of generations?

55

Do not our ancestors still live within us?

Cannot the discerning eye see them

in the turn of a phrase,

the movement of a hand,

or the glance of an eye?

Cannot the discerning ear

hear them come secretly in the night?

Their soft whispers filling our darkened bedrooms?

Are we, ourselves, anything more than this

in some future time and person

whose name we cannot know?

THE FABRIC OF NIGHT AND DAY

I remember when
my eyes grew luminous
and you first welcomed me
into your secret world.

My balance was poor,
the meaning of things
continually escaped me,
I thought we would be together always.

Then you left
and I was insane in darkness.
(Who can abide that darkness
when first it comes?)

Your touch was water,
I had swelled with it.
But in the desert
I shrunk, closed in, dried up.

I learned to grieve there
and - eventually -
to be unafraid.
It was not something I wanted to learn.

When you returned
colors were swept clean.
We talked and laughed long into a night
as bright as if suns were shining.

I thought the desert done,
that you would never leave again,
but I was young and did not know
that there is a coming and going to this.

The water and the sand
are the right and left hand
of the journey.
I shall always be too young.

The knowledge of the luminous world
that I have gathered
as patiently as a squirrel
gathers nuts

fills a thimble
in the kit
you use to sew
the fabric of night and day.

THE MOVEMENT OF GREAT THINGS

There is memory of ocean,

the swelling of waves,

the movement of great things,

just beneath the surface.

My conscious mind staggers,

a part sleeping begins to waken.

What is this great thing?

That has caught us up?

Beloved. . .

Shall we find out together?

Shall we travel to a land

where two-dimensionality does not rule?

Where all that we encounter gazes back at us?

Where directions for the journey

are written in the shape and textures of the land?

Where we see, as far as the eye can touch,

the soul of us opening outward?

Shall we take that step together?

Leave the comfort of the porch,

and strike cross country,

to find the place where the Teacher lives,

the place where the big and the little become one,

the place from which we came long ago,

the place we have heard calling since before we were born?

Shall we go out Beloved

and take the path before us?

Shall we let the perfume of our love

fill all our three bodies?

Come, take my hand,

it has awaited the deep you to fill it,

a length of time too long for remembering.

Come Beloved, let us take this journey together.

My feet are hungry for the first step.

The Taste of Wild Water has been published in an edition of two hundred and fifty copies. Fifty copies, containing an extra holograph poem have been signed and numbered by the author. Twenty-six copies, signed and lettered A-Z, have been reserved for the author's use.

Copy 50

The word is drawn
out of silence
like the sound
out of a stone